Shy Green Fields

Shy Green Fields

Hugh Behm-Steinberg

No Tell Books 2007
Reston, VA

Copyright © 2007 by Hugh Behm-Steinberg

Published by No Tell Books, LLC

notellbooks.org

All rights reserved

ISBN: 978-0-6151-6133-4

Cover Design: Meghan Punschke

Proofreader: Joseph Massey

for Mary

A duet built around the word help. As I am
a man, I cannot talk without my body, my

body keeps leaning into you. I cannot say I
understand the problems of bodies, of translating

your experience into my own. I know the joys
that unbutton you, the bodiliness of what

happens, of surrendering ourselves unto ourselves.

The heart's church, the gravel and plankings,
the angelfood cake in the basement: the angels

hate it and we do too. For there are two of
everything, scapulas, femurs, occasions for

being, etc. The hooks, the legs in your pants,
angels and us, we are not angels and are glad.

(obviously glad) (my hands full of cake).

Creating yellow, getting out of the cold war,
more oranges, we try to talk with only the

clouds listening, those brave little bags, and you
love the linear, and the curved, it loves you

too, and we, curving and curving, the dissolve,
the yes and yes, I make a hoop with my arms,

and there's you, rolling through.

Remember, stay in your body. There's these
all the time things happening, like the clean

house (how did it get that way?) the numbers,
their mapping of the dream world, is folly,

(who put them in that order?) raincoats in
the tropics, would keep the lushness

outside, it cries in, in, in.

Braiding. Proof of life that can explain
what we ourselves can't say. How

the music took over when we sat.
The risky light, all over everybody!

What's coming's almost here! Breaking
the order of things, like here. Being here.

Without dropping your arms so your kid can hug you.

The choreography is deliberate so we know where
to put our feet. What then, these intersections?

Your body is so literal: even unexpected, low, and
out, so sleepiness and sugar. Holy work. Rooted

in the parallels, rooted in the directions, faithfully
showing me how, in what city do you love your

work, that you love me too? Here. This heart.

Great, as in not alone, think about
what's possible, not imaginary but picturing

the uncountable kicks of you, danced,
milk blue, the test results declare we are

all magnetic, that we each have our own
humming sound, a radio frequency, I

am turning into you, tuning into you.

Try to make a body into a city, try to explain
how it might glow in the dark. Say the door

opened out into years. In this city you can
get the life you want, night after night, beside

the VCR glow. You can dream of trapeze artists
and your own private labyrinths. Lead me there.

Lead me through.

About your body, the way your stomach curves
into itself, the bruises and scar tissue that rolls

when I press it. With my hand I skate my way
up your ribcage, around the site, the canula

line, to your breast, your nipple between
my thumb and ring finger. How much is it,

how much is needing you, your body and you.

Being here. It's ok, to be here. The
grit that life has in it. It's mechanical

but I'm used to it. I feel the buzz inside
you, your body and laying beside it.

That enoughness. Someone could
point you in the right direction.

The scale is so much. Fields.

Long, roundabout shapes, the double bend
of your stomach, he remembers your

holiness, reminds you of it, not just songbirds
but the specifics. The spine, vertebrae, his

hand going bump, bump, bump, you saying
scratch here, here. Those luscious specifics,

you could wriggle your body from itself.

God is everywhere, cake is not,
which is why I like it, God says,

and lifts his fork from the plate of
you. He makes it seem like charity.

I don't care what he thinks. I think
about the richness. I too take

enormous bites, here and here.

Ease. In grandeur we were attached we
walked each other down the corridor, and

our footsteps, they were written up in
the newspaper, as a definition of beauty.

Ask questions, the song around our heartbeats.
We said we have no proof, we just picked

it up, like a kiss, some coins, rings.

Your voice is green.
Like water flowing through

a garden, flowerbeds,
laughter. I don't mind the

indirect light, I don't mind
all the work that's left to do.

Doing it right.

Grasps, pushes and swings into space like
forethought, or what is truly clear. That

thing they call the hammer, I want the
reverse, I want the second time, I want

the third. We were lost in the middle but
I had no trouble sleeping. I like your scent,

the tendencies, the exactly how.

Oh, with air, sliding, through the air
until the ear, through the air, into

your head, reminding, in the air, circuiting
until, you have to, you stay up late, becoming

variable, growing that way, tidal, put it all
behind you, these pulling forces, all of them

pulling you.

All the things to love, not out of
selfishness, not minding either.

A sad river, maybe a brook, gone
through, then that too. Maybe enough

just to be green colored, to sleep
in green fields, to linger there in spring.

Go back as far as possible.

Of that space, of wooden measures of that space,
such as the length of your arm, such as a piece of tape

placed and placed, like a man in the house, a man
in the bed, in red sheets, a man getting up to go

to the kitchen, his feet slapping down on the tile;
he's making soup at three in the morning and he's

naked, he pours water as you roll over and sleep.

In the suburbs of the spirit world,
in the aspects, how they were angled

for devoted visitors, their multitudes,
the bell-hops to lug their freight, I thought

oh really, and those bricks, yuck, as for their
treaties, you should talk about me to strangers,

all the kinds, how little is their weight.

It worked at the time as a structure.
Combed through some old knots, or

there were some shadows and chose
to restore what was colorful. Talking

so softly. Candled. People come over
to see how we're doing. Neighboring.

Much among us always.

I live in a water house; it will not evaporate.
Slanting, I know what I'm made of. I can

pivot here. I can walk sideways, I can
swim some. That's my breath inside

my mouth. Some glass, windows, glasses,
some spirals, intervals, cells. There is

another kind of drinking. Wise space.

In the beginning I should have doubted less. Should
have staved off less. Changed my world into tools,

worked on an order that did more than imply order.
After all, I was conceived in joy, like most people,

and I want to multiply happiness, why not? Then
come upon me like I was a structure, through which

I grow more luscious, lusciously.

Binding objects with their names, with what
they're about. To say unhinged would be to

imply there used to be a door. So. There was
a roof *and* a door. To forget what you know

about your body. To weave a garden into you.
There's so much sky wanting in, it is to praise

the infinite that moves, is moving through us.

No one can sleep with them, they climb into the
folds, you can keep them up, they won't even

bite, crawling through, they have sex when they fly,
what should we do? Arcings, that's what we should

do, across beds and tables. You can replace the sky
with sugar, replace the sea with salt, pile the dirt

into mounds, information. Industriousnesses.

Walked along. Into the garden, if
watched, so? Move carelessly as a

dancer resting might walk, buzzing
wooden daylight off the fencing material,

a delight in lemons and a line of ants curling
around them. Say loosened, and repeated,

moving it back and forth in its groove.

I tried to encode
everything I wrote

in mortar. That way.
these centers, their tiles, not just

old circuitry, but grooves, even
paths: brothering, each border

it can bloom past itself, there's time.

Paintcans, shingles, ladders. Water seeps in
through the windows, a flat spot on the roof.

We have ants, we have mold in the bathroom.
The utility room, the study, unfinished, the

drain to the washing machine is held together
with tape. Sunlight on the floor, milk in the fridge,

music to dance with, you to dance to.

I like the way wisteria has to be threaded around
frame structures. I love the smell of lamb. I like

to remember. I like to be formal, as in shapeliness
or planned somehow. Then to lose the plan, and let

what happen. It lets you feel joy, the real thing, not
just its implications. Your eye follows the branch as

it curls around our house, you wanting to follow it too.

So you couldn't tell if it was impossible
or just what you always wanted: you could

taste it, take it inside your mouth, I could
move my whisk so fast it looks like I'm

skipping with just my hands, I got a use for all this air. Meringue,
soft spikes, so exuberant, so funny, so open-armed I'm hard to follow

I have to bring you along with me.

See it through, the slippages.
Gravel covered, sort of hungry.

Like a landlord with all of his leases.
Holding them safe, within my heart.

The blackened one, the one I'm learning
to use again. OK. Carefully. Pulled up the

driveway in a white car, calling you.

A force, sort of a car-shaped force, each day
are the cars, the we or the we plus three.

So I work the above and below buttons
and pulleys, knobs and hooks, nurturing

the spark, the lovely little spark. I fall asleep
on the tilework, and the force it comes not once

but as you are, what you carry inside you.

Every time they pull me I
want to get on with it.

So, scrubbed pots. Did some jobs.
The yard work. Slices of toast.

And you don't know. And time
turning over; what you say

is too hard to know.

I can feel. That it's me, with my
arms around your hips. Half sung,

that kind of moving. You could be
the sea road, you are the one who

points. The sleepy houses, maybe
touch my elbow. Seamless, as I am led

into this world. This understanding, felt.

Skew points, even before you've begun. Inscribed
with the sitting, move a long low chest from one

side of the house. Was so careful, such a great clockmaker.
He might be whispering. It was the work he wanted, he

wanted it placed, he wanted to live in it. Live there.
Without fear, ascending as roses often do, in their

season, understanding time. Crossing that now with now.

Is the way to. Is it a switching? Places,
continental, a kind of wilderness, I'm not

afraid to read it that way. Sleep on rocks,
the sun's so warm. To be just one, of ones.

I am beloved. I am loved. Show me the
thickets. To be without power, only increase.

Where the materials peer out. You and you.

I said this including myself so you can
come nestle with me, we'll turn all the

appliances off and watch the tomatoes grow.
Let the contexts shift without us, for there's

a point in the song where it sounds like
the CD player is skipping, it sounds like

beautiful rain blessing everything it touches.

Portrait with sky. Handling clouds.
Does it seem you're in love? Does

your love make the seasons subdivide?
The clouds go over there, next to the

window. When I am naked, the little
hairs stretch out, they brush against

your skin, also resembling clouds.

Scribbles, a man lying face down in a pile.
He was a fool, he blessed the wrong son.

So then, chipped, a little sky. A wing, two.
A treaty against sinking would come in handy.

You won't make that mistake. That's the point,
it wasn't pointless, you make the old man float

so you won't see yourself in him.

Nobody would think, there was a point where
enough pressure would let you through, a

part of you, and the rest, what you never wanted,
it would be left behind. Therefore, rising up

is the garden, where the emperor, sitting, sits.
Starting out of joy and complexity, you go though,

and therefore the sky, it is full of secrets.

The sky has grains. I have something to do.
An iris stalk bent over, the weight of its blossoms.

I can be a king of white smoke, I can canter.
There's so much weather my gestures blow

away. I replace them with more deliberate
gestures: this is the rolling pin, the drive home,

the key, turning, turning and turning.

Earth and sky are married.
Door and window married too.

Aaron and Bronwyn are already married.
But we're getting married too.

I used to believe in ironies, I would
sniff for the underlying complexities.

Starting and startling, now we're two.

Actually brave, only appearing tentative
as a kind of slyness, some soft dust;

you can see you, peeling you off of
you, your voice, reaching out, the branches,

the radio glow of the sky, a possibility of ticking,
see – it was hardly known, so we hung back,

oiled unto ourselves, budding green shoots, sleep.

Firlight. Leafed. The mouth of the earth
in which the moon is swallowed and

abides each day. I thought about the
invisible. That doesn't mean I could

see it, not even the outlines, but to
hear it speak, the mouth making new

bodies, softly.

Let's do the sleep, let's do the stumble,
let's park, early high, early green, new.

Not part, pleased, grassy even, shirtless,
shirt left on the floor, marvelous, all sorts

of phrasings. Say I was branched, the moon
was milkblue above me, but the grass called

me down to you, so I reached.

As broad as meteors, classical, almost in
the sky, taking up my place. Someone

accounts for each button on the shirt
you wear. Lots happens. Leonids. This

is later. I put it on, slipping it down over
my arms. This will last forever, won't it? In

that corner of the sky there, flying down.

It has no wing space, the audience is right there;
they carried in themselves, they liking that.

Observes, the language of strangers, with such
concentration. We were unsteady, the river

beneath the river all raggling saying I love
you I will not be judicious with my body.

So, now, we look, in warm air, a softness.

Joined in two. Kind of liking that. I fell in love
with my limits and getting into my body

I found something to talk about. I'm embarrassed,
but like everyone else I'm working on a novel and

like most people it's stuck in my head. The world
won't just be. It narrates. Has plots, characters.

Memorize the skies. The skies know you already.

Showed such pushing. Because we
want freedom and our passion collects

so much besides feeling. We'd like to
keep love singular, and not just formally

but also in the birth of texts, or of crows,
the sense time has stopped for us, love

draws with it what is next.

Like how a book continues to think and
not just record thinking, aligning all these

fractures, sand, to go on talking, sure of
this, of how this goes, like how each of

the blindnesses has a reader, a spinning voice,
a fated Braille. There are weightless places.

How we get so bright.

Just now, some lettering. Then again,
could take some time to dry. The sweet

hookings, the solar radiation, your kind
of holiness, now set in columns, those

consonants, from what they ought to
mean to how you take them to heart,

it is how you hear it.

Or at the time, the misses, the hand upon the
various switches, you pulled up on the heavenly

knob until it said open and I said what is right
and wondrous, only without so many consonants,

I mean I finally meant all the vowels I could think of.
And my name, it was no longer my name, it was

that good, I couldn't even remember my name.

The inside commentator, his quiet delivery, warm,
fits the instructions to the speaker. About the words:

they are meant to be read. A serpentine line, adults
and children, ages and sizes, different callings,

straightforward joy, I couldn't say it myself without
you. We formed a wedge with the dancers, who can't

speak yet, you and me the words they're going to say.

The heart's clerk, the records of joy,
it took an entire team with a lot of

geniuses, the slip of paper, the missing
file. I love a good conspiracy, I love

fighting your bureaucracy, the you you
mean and the you you say, the minutes

they go back, they point the way through.

A book coming out of its binding, fraying
cardboard corners. Informal, ok, is the way to.

What opens up is consciousness, you bother
to use your heart, your blood goes around

without you wanting it to. Is it a switching,
is there something exchanged, a continent?

My oxygen, my wilderness, the pages of.

Are incomplete. Over the rooftops.
Bookfilled. So distractions, even flaws,

and instead of happiness, things are
open to happiness, you can decide how

you will live. In the path you on
your route towards. Your hand, its

fingers curling around.

Not words, but a promise nonetheless, made
out of my own body heat, flakes of skin, hair,

clothes sorted and washed, the dishes in the
cabinet, the shelves, 32 shopping bags of books;

the completion of my gestures as they
become acts and set the true ideal of

a full and reasonable life.

It matters what you want, for you are not
the mouth, you are the reasons, the way

experience works its way into the poem
and the poem justifies the way we treat

each other. You fold my plum shirt.
It goes in the chifforobe. When I get

dressed this is how I feel in my body.

If the world would fit, it would
belong like a letter in your hand.

I pointed and pointed, like a
kid at the zoo, eager, publicly.

Rising in white shapes, envelopes
like snow or counting the

days till it snows.

Perhaps by being called, we kept arriving.
We were written instead of filmed. The writing

trails upward, resembles lovers in their
entanglements, whole paragraphs of you.

When stuck, you should write about the
moon. I don't need to be chosen I was

never separate from you.

It's said cranes need lots of room. How
do they exist so far apart and stay together?

I couldn't stand it, to not be able to see
your body, to not be part of you out of

some genetic modesty. I have trouble
staying asleep without you. I belong to

another world.

Over hundreds of years, stone and soil
organize themselves into patterns,

or lifted, lifting. Sure. The visible, the shine
of it is green and its own kind of knowing.

My other face, maybe I was a man inside
of myself, I didn't just find myself beside

you. Conversant, as birds here do.

To let more slip in. It was fruitful, generous.
Maybe it poured out, like a dog in the corn.

Maybe the roots or the sap are depictions
of friendship. Through to the stone. And so much

air, perhaps I was the scripture, the fluttering,
the wetness entwined in the ancient fields

where we find each other, in the gaping world, here.

Approached then loitered some around.
Botanied the self and all its horticultures.

Weedily, strewn lands, folds and more.
A body belonging to another body who

uses it carefully to break all kinds of codes.
And to stroll with, about outside on walks.

Snails, small birds, raccoons, argentine ants.

Significances. A man with his mouth open.
Me saying o. Aloes, scales and fens. The eye

it skims over these things. We used to sit.
I will never ruin this. I will have four means

to find me, and let the stories pour, from kindness
is the prayer call. You know what you can do.

Asleep in shy green fields, rolling into you.

Randy, not staying put. Digging
up into you with my roots.

In our life is our life, wanting to
include the advances, the oranges

you want to chew. See me as a man.
See me spread like branches, raindroplets

as constellations, with stars.

Walk around, like in a zoo. Unexpectedness.
In from the cold, around the puddle, shy green

are the markings, are the scents I made, I'm
gonna get emptied of all structure now, I'm

gonna take my skeleton out for a swim, we're
gonna clear out the garden. Sleepy-eyed, then

climbing, in gardens, these marvels, roundnesses.

Revelations! The wild snorts angels make!
You'll never step on the ground again!

The name, it is so literal, the shadow has
six spokes, the arms they are so radiant

you'll never walk in this country again!
You'll lie down in iris petals! Wheels vs.

spheres! Defending the *world* from the *world*.

What brings us? What air, pearls?
Under pale rain, root puller, weightlessness.

Soaked, so didn't break. It was pearled,
also winged, and I could wait for hours.

Enveloped in it. Only finally, luminously, in-
sist upon an unfolding. Roses. This scattered

ground of cloverflowers, bundled tight.

A word, which means the edge of something.
Think of what you want, such certainty, such

cool reposes. I used to hate this kind of work,
it reminded me of childhood, weeding the Russian

olive trees, poisonous work. With some subjects
I am only a burden, everything I know only

gets me in trouble. Weeds grow out of my mouth.

Little rectangles become a person. I like that.
Your mouth, the kisses of your mouth, they

go here, they are *planted*. Could even think
of my body as a garden, I mean I have these

plots. Who's to say what I'm made of? Not
rectangles, certainly, but lines, furrows, that

curve, they almost tangle, like vines or hair.

Formal, a sprawlingness, tonal
as in using your tongue, you

could rattle saints, you
could invent new forms of sex, you

could peel me like an orange,
my sticky white pith, my strings,

my sweet wants.

It comes. Say so. Like a well shaped
mouth could say so. As if saying so

is based on mouths, and not on what
holds you. Yellow birds in your lungs.

So you sing. Sing of feeling cool, of
looking good, no one watching. So, cool.

Eating the entire carton of ice cream.

Here are plastic duck tongues. These are
the artificial teeth for a boar. Such versions!

They thread breath between us and roses with steel
needles, they prefer bone and sinew. Nylon thread.

I am friendly. I have trouble keeping secrets.
You can bare your teeth. You know your own

body, the one you love. Which is before you.

Mansions, turning to you.
I'm exhausted. So it tastes sweet.

I'm staying in New York City.
I go for a walk every Sunday

and I do my research. Faced, suspended
in leaves, pale green, left ear, dark green.

Going to bed with a copper taste in my mouth.

I like black. I like to linger. I
am all sorts of invitations. I

don't want to be buried, not yet,
I am feeling too carnal, I want to

be fed to the mouth of all numbers,
I want to liberate the world from

counting its hate teeth.

Maybe I have a skeleton, maybe I was
pieced together from various parts

which recall us, how we love each other
as we resembled elephants; I love elephants.

Some people don't get it: I'm not one of them.
I represent the freedom of animals. I walk

around in a giant body. I get to do that.

You, you hook me, I like it that way.
I couldn't keep this as a secret. That

in my heart is the zoo. The cages and
the animals and the overwhelmingness of

it all, you just want to stick your hand in
to pet the tiger. Not just now, not just once.

The heart's fur. That dangerous softness.

Swanned. Hipping, so passionate I
felt unmade, unbecoming, spun upward

turned, I came back right, I took my
time, gladly cleaned the floor, sanded

it smooth, verethaned, slick, three
layers, you could glide, like a swan,

how it does what it wants to do.

We thought they were two ravens,
but one got up off the rabbit and

both were brown and grease black,
their heads bald and pink. They could

hardly be bothered. There is such abundance
here, there are so many more of them,

you see two and a hundred come.

Oxen, the same frustrating answer
from some formless era, or from nothing at all,

born, endless. Maybe crouched in the night fields,
where the night grows, the dark blooms, with luck

there is some happiness in this. The sound of their lowing,
the completed work, may it be that way and not

to tear it up, alphabetized packets of seeds, some flowers.

Larger frames. Worked around the idea in different
ways. Are the wounds, which try to heal themselves,

we try to help this happen. A garden, outwardly.
The land smells like rain, the ghosts, their heartbeats:

I know what's right, I keep getting pulled into
smaller and smaller pieces. This is my best thought,

I thought of it first.

I love the looking, to see over, see giraffes,
to pet the giraffe from a platform, the sexuality

of feeding them, their long black tongues.
How enviable! The old one, the oldest one,

these luscious attachments, you are the way
the sweat of your hands taste. Full of salt,

knowing. You are the sugar you carry inside you.

Nothing happens. The days sing nothing,
no one you know, now what do you want?

I can't believe I'm blushing! The what you
want, some snow, staying here, I ran through

the stones, I ran with my dogs, I didn't get
tired, I wasn't shrouded, I wasn't lonely, I

felt my heart, plump and happy.

Living in the same box, the world with
dirt (soils! clays, even, in spots) untidy

and reliable, thick with worminess, useful
(of what use) and covered, the scary bugs

tumbling on top of each other, toylike, through
the eggshells, the eggplant I chop in half

with a shovel.

Cocks its head. Joined by another. So
it is humid, and there's nowhere else

to walk to, it extends its wings, perhaps
that is its way of thinking. What is there

to think about? The birds trade places,
their beaks wet with rabbit blood. Wildness

is here. It has a use for you.

To anyone who was frightened. To start.
To be chopped up and fed to the right wolves.

To explain why you are free, and what you
did with your chances. To run headfirst.

To know your worth by who is chasing you.
There's a reason why these things happen.

I thought of luck. I won't need it anymore.

Then I will move on, like sisters,
twice as much as sisters, advancing

the solvency of myself into very
specific others, until we are exquisite:

then we will train birds to sing like we do,
like a favorite book with three pages extra,

the better to keep it in our hearts.

Not knowing their names we didn't see them.
Not knowing what to call them we pointed.

At first we thought, a rabbit, then look at all
the rabbits, look at the woodchucks, then look

at the deer, the squirrels, the trees left standing,
the farms left over, the enormous houses scattered,

the roads of us, how we got here, what keeps us.

Walk over the snow
or carried, carrying. Nervous.

The invisible sorrow, the shine of it
white unknowing, maybe the dogs want you.

My louder voice, maybe I was a child
in the mouth of another child, I'm letting myself.

It's such an old, loving song.

A man is just a joke and if his fingers
were glue, his name would be glue and

if his bones were glue, we wouldn't know
what to call him, maybe Stucky. But what

if he wore stylish shoes, what if he knew
more than he let on? Something about the

world getting more slippery...

Who lived around the corner and smelled
the smoke and knew it was wood burning.

Who felt a light coming on as a lover calling.
And the joint between the thumb and palm,

praise it. You'll never know, you'll never
know. What is most important. There it is,

half sung, sharing joy, these lineaments.

What the siren sang of. Sang of
fires. What people are in a rush to

save, what the world even more
quickly gives away. Nobody

listens like you do. Hereness. The
next life, green like the one you get

to live all over again.

Suspended, sometimes, between pairs,
undulating, sometimes, unbreaking, yes,

under ourselves, sometimes, we read all about
it with our skin, we read human joy with our

hands, we pay attention, the plot twists, we
let regret slip off, we're unsleeping, very here.

In the pleasures of our own sung breath.

These dances have a past, but how did they get
here? They try to explain themselves as landscape,

as that which moves like a coiled one-armed
handstand, as bounces and curves, as sudden,

straight-up jumps. The dancers ask us to vibrate
our knees, that our torsos would acquire accents,

French, Chinese, Western American, drawling steps.

Soars, while people in hats and scarves
pass you. It's not fair to just leave me

there; with two dancers tattooed on my
leg, I hadn't thought one of them would

come to mean you. It marks me as a man
who gazes, but I am also part of a tribe

that does more than look.

We were investigating something
very seriously. The ability to surprise.

So, watchful. Watching over us. These
faithful systems. So, we sat in the air.

A piece of you lingers inside of you.
It is the cave a dancer makes with her body.

How we were loved, or what we try to.

Weak from sleeping without you, my
arrival is bonewhite and welcomed by

the patriarchs, for they have been hunted, they
don't remember where the money went,

the silt in the causeway was unintended, and
the night air, the poor, it's true I thought, blown

and released, I didn't stop for them.

What causes persons to become people?
To lie flat and then stick up? There was

a trap but we avoided it. There were favorites
we avoided them too. The animal shadow of course,

the promise you grow into, of course. To hide
in the dark. I leave something in myself, I

got younger just thinking about it!

To be a piece of someone, to
find yourself in somebody else.

Moving from a scratch on wood
to reading the oldest scratch there is.

Sitting on the table, your legs
kick around in little circles.

It matters what you want.

And still, and still. Is so complicated we turn around,
this way and that; there is more, it was practiced.

A longing, to lose yourself, in. Something so
new it hurts to hold it inside you. So, no stones.

No ice, no restlessness. In your hand, the leaf,
in your hand, each secret, and the world it is

so round with you in it.

Index

a full and reasonable life, 62
all the kinds, how little is their weight, 25
am turning into you, tuning into you, 13
and released, I didn't stop for them, 103
and there's you, rolling through, 9
and therefore the sky, it is full of secrets, 45
another kind of drinking. Wise space, 27
another world, 66
around in a giant body. I get to do that, 82
as constellations, with stars, 71
Asleep in shy green fields, rolling into you, 70

beautiful rain blessing everything it touches, 42
bodies, softly, 49
body, the one you love. Which is before you, 79
but as you are, what you carry inside you, 37

climbing, in gardens, these marvels, roundnesses, 72
counting its hate teeth, 81
curve, they almost tangle, like vines or hair, 76

days till it snows, 64
Doing it right, 20
draws with it what is next, 54
dressed this is how I feel in my body, 63
driveway in a white car, calling you, 36

Eating the entire carton of ice cream, 78
enormous bites, here and here, 18

felt my heart, plump and happy, 89
fingers curling around, 61
French, Chinese, Western American, drawling steps, 100

gets me in trouble. Weeds grow out of my mouth, 75
Go back as far as possible, 23
Going to bed with a copper taste in my mouth, 80
got younger just thinking about it!, 104
ground of cloverflowers, bundled tight, 74

half sung, sharing joy, these lineaments, 97
happens, of surrendering ourselves unto ourselves, 7
how it does what it wants to do, 84
how much is needing you, your body and you, 15
How we get so bright, 55
How we were loved, or what we try to, 102

I grow more luscious, lusciously, 28
I have to bring you along with me, 35
I thought of it first, 87
I thought of luck. I won't need it anymore, 92
In the pleasures of our own sung breath, 99
into mounds, information. Industriousnesses, 30
into this world. This understanding, felt, 39
is here. It has a use for you, 91

is too hard to know, 38
it can bloom past itself, there's time, 32
it curls around our house, you wanting to follow it too, 34
it is how you hear it, 56
It matters what you want, 105
it up, like a kiss, some coins, rings, 19
It's such an old, loving song, 95

knowing. You are the sugar you carry inside you, 88

Lead me through, 14

me down to you, so I reached, 50
Memorize the skies. The skies know you already, 53
moving it back and forth in its groove, 31
Much among us always, 26
music to dance with, you to dance to, 33
My oxygen, my wilderness, the pages of, 60
my sweet wants, 77

naked, he pours water as you roll over and sleep, 24
never separate from you, 65

(obviously glad) (my hands full of cake), 8
oiled unto ourselves, budding green shoots, sleep, 48
outside, it cries in, in, in, 10

pulling you, 22

season, understanding time. Crossing that now with now, 40
So, now, we look, in warm air, a softness, 52
so round with you in it, 106
so you won't see yourself in him, 44
Snails, small birds, raccoons, argentine ants, 69

speak yet, you and me the words they're going to say, 58
spheres! Defending the *world* from the *world*, 73
Starting and startling, now we're two, 47

that corner of the sky there, flying down, 51
that does more than look, 101
that good, I couldn't even remember my name, 57
the better to keep it in our hearts, 93
The heart's fur. That dangerous softness, 83
the infinite that moves, is moving through us, 29
the key, turning, turning and turning, 46
the roads of us, how we got here, what keeps us, 94
The scale is so much. Fields, 16
the tendencies, the exactly how, 21
they go back, they point the way through, 59
to live all over again, 98
to tear it up, alphabetized packets of seeds, some flowers, 86

Where the materials peer out. You and you, 41
where we find each other, in the gaping world, here, 68
with a shovel, 90
Without dropping your arms so your kid can hug you, 11
work, that you love me too? Here. This heart, 12
world getting more slippery..., 96

you. Conversant, as birds here do, 67
you could wriggle your body from itself, 17
you see two and a hundred come, 85
your skin, also resembling clouds, 43

Acknowledgments

Grateful acknowledgment is made to the editors and publishers of the following journals in which portions of this book have previously appeared: *Boston Review, Can We Have Our Ball Back?, Epoch, Fine Madness, Fence, Five Fingers Review, 5_Trope, 42opus, Forklift, Ohio, No Tell Motel, Slope* and *Sonora Review.*

I would like to thank the National Endowment for the Arts for a poetry fellowship that supported me during the start of this project. Thanks also to Denise Newman, whose request for an essay on gardens was the prompt for several passages and the title. Much thanks also to Meghan Punschke for the beautiful cover, and to Joe Massey for his close reading of the manuscript. Many thanks to my teachers, friends, colleagues and neighbors. Finally, most deluxe and extravagant thanks to the fabulous and foxy Reb Livingston for her support, hard work, advice and encouragement in the publication of this book.

About the Author

Hugh Behm-Steinberg received degrees from Johns Hopkins and the University of Arizona and was a Wallace Stegner Fellow at Stanford University. Recipient of an NEA Creative Writing Fellowship, he lives in Berkeley, California with his wife Mary. He teaches at California College of the Arts, where he edits the journal *1111*.

Also by No Tell Books

2008

Personations, by Karl Parker

2007

The Bedside Guide to No Tell Motel - 2nd Floor, editors Reb Livingston
      & Molly Arden
The Myth of the Simple Machines, by Laurel Snyder
Harlot, by Jill Alexander Essbaum
Never Cry Woof, by Shafer Hall

2006

The Bedside Guide to No Tell Motel, editors Reb Livingston
      & Molly Arden
Elapsing Speedway Organism, by Bruce Covey
The Attention Lesson, by PF Potvin
Navigate, Amelia Earhart's Letters Home, by Rebecca Loudon
Wanton Textiles, by Reb Livingston & Ravi Shankar

notellbooks.org